Skills Map

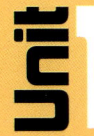

Unit 1 Getting organised

Learn some basic principles of academic writing: essay structure; analysing essay questions; brainstorming ideas and issues.

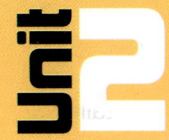

Unit 2 Getting started

Understand how to plan your writing. Learn to create effective introductions and write thesis statements.

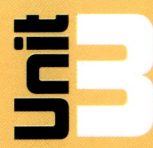

Unit 3 The body of the essay

Practise arranging your arguments in a logical sequence. Learn effective paragraphing. Practise supporting your arguments.

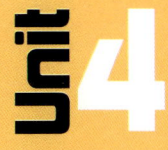

Unit 4 Summaries and conclusions

Learn how to close your argument and draw conclusions.

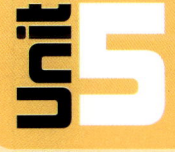

Unit 5 Academic style and register

Practise using appropriate language: formal vs. informal style and some important aspects of academic written language.

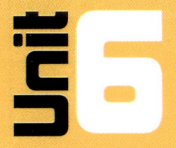

Unit 6 Guidelines for the future

Remember some important points: lecturer expectations; producing a detailed essay outline. Study a model essay.

Destination: Essay Writing

Getting organised

At the end of this unit you will:
- understand more about the requirements of writing an academic essay;
- have learnt how to produce a clear outline.

Task 1 Basic principles of essay writing

There are several different types of academic essay. For example, you might have to write:

- a descriptive essay
- an argument essay
- an analytical essay
- an evaluative essay
- a personal experience essay
- a reflective essay

Some essays may be a mixture of different approaches and types, but you need to be clear what sort of essay you are writing.

1.1 Match the following titles with the essay type as above. Note that sometimes you will need to combine categories.

Title	Type
Using your personal experience, describe a particularly interesting cultural encounter.	
What are the main arguments for and against the implementation of very high rates of taxation?	
How good do you think the author is at creating the characters in this story? Analyse the characterisation and give examples.	
The most efficient form of transport is the train. Discuss.	
Using the statistics in the accompanying table, write an analytical description of the rise in the number of British households.	
The European Union is already far too big. Discuss.	
Learning a language is one of the best forms of educational activity. Do you agree?	

Task: Essay Writing - Unit 1 - Getting organised

1.2 Whatever the essay type, the structure of an essay is generally similar. The purpose is to help the reader understand what the writer wants to say.

Write down what you think form the three main parts of an academic essay.

a)

b)

c)

1.3 In pairs or groups, discuss the following aspects of an essay. Make notes of your discussion and present the conclusions to the class.

The introduction:	What is it for? What makes a good introduction?
The essay structure:	What is a paragraph? How do you show where a paragraph begins and ends? How do you decide the order of paragraphs?
The conclusion:	What is it for? What makes a good conclusion?

1.4 The purpose of this module is to improve your essay-writing skills. As a starting point, it would be useful to evaluate your current skills in specific areas.

Do the questionnaire below. Mark your competence in each area on a scale of 1 to 5 (1 = poor, 5 = excellent). Compare your answers with another student.

Skill	Score
Writing correct and accurate English	
Planning an outline of an essay	
Drafting and redrafting my writing	
Editing and proofreading	
Organising information	
Organising my time	
Finding and using source material	
Paraphrasing other people's words	

Note: You will be able to think about the basic principles of academic writing in more depth in Unit 6. However, it is useful at this stage to think about what you can do already.

Task 2 Analysing the essay question

2.1 The instruction verbs in the box below are commonly used in essay questions. Think about their meaning. Then discuss your ideas with a partner.

> identify   analyse   describe   comment   compare   discuss   evaluate   exemplify

2.2 Read the following essay question. Find and underline the key ideas it asks you to write about.

> Discuss the problems associated with traffic congestion. Suggest possible solutions and evaluate their effectiveness.

2.3 What *exactly* does the essay question want you to do? Circle the instruction verbs in the question. Then think carefully about the kind of essay you need to write. Discuss your conclusions with the rest of the class.

2.4 Ask yourself questions related to the three key elements of the essay. Begin with *Discuss the problems associated with traffic congestion.* Think about the three questions below. Then add one more question.

a) What exactly is traffic congestion?

b) Where would you find traffic congestion?

c) What are the main causes of traffic congestion?

d) _____

congestion caused by bad weather

congestion caused by maintenance work

congestion caused by weight of traffic

6 Task: Essay Writing - Unit 1 - Getting organised

2.5 **With another student, discuss the rest of the question:** Suggest possible solutions and evaluate their effectiveness, using the same procedure as above.

2.6 Discuss your questions and answers in groups. Present your conclusions to the class.

2.7 In groups, discuss possible solutions to any aspect of traffic congestion. Choose three possible solutions and write them on a piece of paper. Exchange your solutions with another group and evaluate the effectiveness of the other group's solutions.

Task 3 Brainstorming ideas

Brainstorming involves *free association*, or rapidly generating ideas on a topic. Try these two different ways of brainstorming.

Free writing
This is where you quickly write down every idea you have that could be relevant to the topic. You can write a list or draw a spidergram. The aim is to produce lots of ideas, so the form is not important. You do not need to worry about correct spelling or grammar – it is the ideas that are important.

Group brainstorming
This is where all the members of a group contribute their own ideas on the topic, 'bouncing' their ideas off each other.

3.1 **Use free writing to brainstorm the following topic:**

Transporting goods by road.

You have two minutes.

3.2 **Now carry out a group brainstorming activity.**

   a) Start individually. Think about the topic Banning lorries from towns and cities. Accept any ideas that come into your head.

   b) Work in groups. Appoint a chairperson to write down ideas. Then brainstorm the topic.

Task 4 Organising your ideas

Now that you have a set of ideas, they need putting together in an organised way. One method is to use a mind map to try to represent your ideas in a visual form. This can be very useful when you want to quickly see the relationship between your main topic, main ideas and supporting ideas (see essay title, Task 2.2).

You write the main topic in the middle of the page and place the main ideas around it, connected with lines or arrows. Similarly, you write the supporting ideas around the main ideas, connected with lines or arrows.

4.1 Below is a skeleton mind map of the essay topic you are developing. Complete the mind map with your ideas so far.

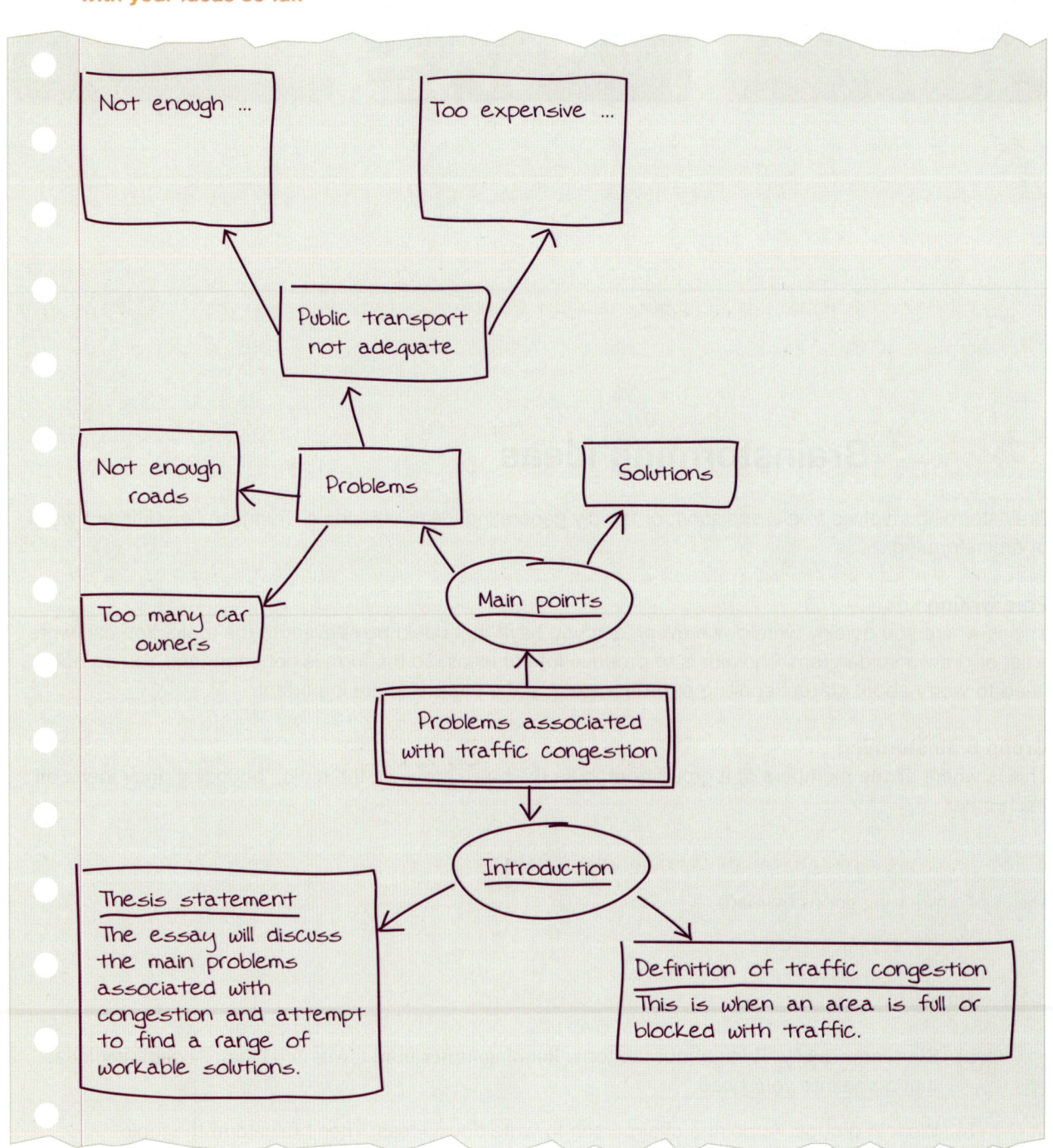

4.2　Using your mind maps, work in groups to discuss the possible content of your essay, the introduction and main points.

> **Reflect**
>
> Think about the ideas you have discussed in this unit. How have they changed your attitude to essay writing?
>
> Apply these insights to an essay you have to write, or think of a topic you are interested in and imagine you are going to write about it. Reflect on the process you will go through, from understanding the question to organising your ideas. Think about how to ensure you fully answer the essay question set by your tutors.

Student notes for Unit 1

2 Getting started

At the end of this unit you will:
- be better equipped to start writing an essay;
- understand how to write a thesis statement;
- have ideas on how to make the introduction interesting for the reader.

Task 1 What to include

Once you have begun to organise your ideas in a logical way, you need to decide:
- how to structure your essay;
- how (and where) to include these ideas.

For example, you need to make decisions about the main sections of your essay.

1.1 You might want to include the following points in your essay on traffic congestion. Think about the importance of each item in the list. Label them I, U or NI (important, useful, not important). Add any other items or topics you can think of.

   a) A definition of traffic congestion.
   b) An explanation of the causes of traffic congestion.
   c) Your views on traffic congestion.
   d) A list of solutions to the problem.
   e) Examples of traffic problems in your hometown.
   f) Arguments in favour of or against possible solutions.
   g) _____
   h) _____
   i) _____

1.2 Decide in which order the ideas should appear in the essay. Which ones will you need to spend most time on? Compare your ideas with another student.

Task 2 Information gathering

In academic writing it is not enough to use your own ideas without any supporting evidence. It is essential to include relevant information from academic sources to give them 'academic weight'. You should obtain this information by thoroughly researching the topic, using a variety of sources.

It is important to make clear notes of any information you find. You can then use this information, with references, to support your argument. (See *TASK*, Module 10: *Research & referencing*.) Keep a record of all your sources when you collect the information, as it is easier to do this at the time, rather than later.

2.1 Discuss possible sources with another student. Write what you think will be your four main sources of information.

Sources of information

_____

_____

_____

_____

2.2 Number the following points in the order of difficulty for you.

_____ Finding appropriate references

_____ Paraphrasing in your own words

_____ Understanding how much use to make of external sources

_____ Referencing in an appropriate way

2.3 Discuss your answers as a class.

Task 3 Arousing interest: The introduction

The introduction acts as a window to the rest of your writing. A good introduction should make your reader want to read your work. You can encourage interest by using a variety of different techniques. For example, you can use one or more of the following:

a) a surprising or interesting fact

b) a question

c) a quotation

d) a definition

e) some important background information

Unit 2 - Getting started - Task: Essay Writing   11

3.1 Which of the above, a) – e), has the author used in the introduction to an essay entitled:

The education system in your country?

> According to a recent survey, a significant proportion of the population in my country has serious literacy problems.

3.2 Look at the four essay titles below. Think of a sentence to use as an introduction to each one, using any of the above, a) – e). Try to interest the reader so as to encourage him/her to read the rest of the essay.

   a) Family structure in your country

   b) The criminal justice system in your country

   c) Imports and exports to and from your country

   d) Transportation in your country

Task 4 Writing a thesis statement

An introduction should also contain information on how you will develop the topic in the essay title. You write this in the **thesis statement**, a statement of your standpoint or the view taken in the essay. It should be concise and convincing. Your thesis is the controlling idea of your essay that you will develop in the main body.

You normally follow the thesis statement with a clear indication of how you will structure the main body of your essay in support of your thesis statement.

4.1 The controlling ideas can be stated in many different ways. Identify the controlling ideas of the following thesis statements.

   a) The criminal justice system in my country functions in a variety of ways.

   b) Although the Big Bang Theory is widely accepted, it will probably never be proved, and it therefore leaves a number of difficult and unanswered questions.

   c) The key to coping with the rise in sea levels is education on its effects and the accurate forecasting of its hazards.

4.2 How do you think the rest of the essay will be developed in each case? What areas will be covered? Continue each statement with a sentence outlining the structure of the essay, beginning: 'This essay will ...'.

12 Task: Essay Writing - Unit 2 - Getting started

4.3 Look back at the ideas you brainstormed in Unit 1 on traffic congestion. What is your own view about possible solutions to the problems? Identify your main idea and write it as the controlling idea in a single sentence. This will be your thesis statement.

4.4 What will you focus on? How will you develop your thesis in the main body of your essay? Write a follow-on sentence beginning: 'This essay will ...'.

Task 5 An effective introduction

An introduction should generally move from the general to the specific. The following example is an introduction to an essay about the problems associated with urban overcrowding.

5.1 Arrange the five sentences in the correct order.

a) _____ As a result of this migration, modern-day cities face a number of serious problems related to overcrowding.

b) _____ People were therefore drawn towards living in towns and cities for simple economic reasons.

c) _____ The purpose of this essay is to identify solutions to these problems of urban overcrowding and attempt to evaluate their feasibility.

d) _____ The most critical problems include homelessness, inadequate healthcare and education, unemployment, and knock-on effects such as rising crime and drug abuse.

e) _____ The twentieth century saw a major increase in the world's population and, at the same time, the emergence of a society driven by the forces of economics and industry.

5.2 Discuss the following three questions with another student.

a) Mark the general statements G. How do they attempt to interest the reader?

b) Mark the thesis statement with a tick. How do you expect the rest of the essay to be organised?

c) What are the minimum number of paragraphs you would expect in this essay? What can you predict about their content?

5.3 The questions below can act as a checklist when writing an introduction. Look at the checklist and think about how helpful this will be for you.

_____ Is it likely to interest the reader? Why?

_____ Does it start with a general statement related to the topic and gradually become more specific?

_____ Is there a thesis statement that tells the reader what the essay will be about? Can you easily identify it?

_____ Does the introduction give an overview of the essay structure?

_____ Are ideas clearly linked between sentences or is it sometimes confusing?

_____ Does it include a definition? Do you think a definition is necessary or would be helpful?

5.4 Using the checklist as your criterion, evaluate the following introduction to a student's essay. Complete the table of strengths and weaknesses below the introduction.

The advantages and disadvantages of genetically modified crops

New developments in the field of genetically modified (GM) agriculture are reported almost daily as exciting new discoveries are made. These new developments have generally been welcomed by consumers. Recently, however, people have begun to realise how rapidly GM agriculture is spreading, so questions are being asked about its effects on our environment and health. Needless to say, farmers generally feel that high production levels and top-quality crops are more important than the possible negative side effects. In the light of such advantages, the influence of GM agriculture on the environment and on our health is, in my opinion, unimportant.

Strengths	Weaknesses

14 Task: Essay Writing - Unit 2 - Getting started

5.5 Choose one of the following essay titles and write a possible introduction. Discuss the content and structure with another student before you start writing.

- Food additives should be banned. Discuss.
- What are the main benefits of investing money in space research?
- Euthanasia should be made legal. Discuss.
- Outline the different types of alternative energy sources.
- What would you do to improve the lives of the elderly in your country?

Essay writing: points to remember
- Planning and organisation are key skills.
- Keep a close eye on your title: always answer the question.
- Word processing is very useful. For example, you can change text or move sections about very easily. (See Module 7: *Introduction to IT Skills*.)
- Keep a note as you go along of all references or sources that you use.
- Redrafting is an essential skill.

Reflect

Sometimes writers prefer to write the introduction after they have finished writing the essay. Bearing in mind what you have been studying, do you think this is a good idea? Why or why not?

Think about the main criteria for a good introduction and why they are so important. Can you add any more? Reflect on ways that you can make these criteria important for you and how they will help you throughout your student life.

Student notes for Unit 2

Unit 3 — The body of the essay

At the end of this unit you will:
- have a clear idea of how to structure the main part of an academic essay;
- know how to plan and write effective paragraphs.

Remember, if you want to write a successful academic essay, you need to have the following:

- an outline plan
- a clear structure
- a strong introduction
- logical and meaningful paragraphs
- a development of an argument or discussion
- a conclusion

The organisation of your essay will depend to some extent on what sort of essay you are writing. The body of your essay can be arranged in various logical ways, for example:

- Reasons for and reasons against
- Causes followed by effects
- Problems followed by solutions

Task 1 Paragraph organisation

1.1 Decide whether the statements below are true or false. Discuss your answers as a class.

a) _____ Each main idea should be presented separately in a new paragraph.

b) _____ Each paragraph in the body of your essay will usually begin with a topic sentence stating the main idea of the paragraph.

c) _____ The topic sentence should be followed by several sentences which support the main idea.

d) _____ To add support or evidence, you should use examples, figures or statistics.

e) _____ You should always use quotations to support your ideas.

f) _____ You should have a strong concluding sentence in each paragraph to link the reader back to the topic sentence or provide a link to the next paragraph or section.

1.2 Look at the following extract from a descriptive essay on the origins of Coca-Cola. Can you divide the text into paragraphs?

The first episode in the Coca-Cola story is an important part of the rise of capitalism in the United States of America. Towards the end of the nineteenth century, America gradually began to transform itself from a nation of farmers to a city-based industrialised society. The industrial revolution was epitomised by new communications and the arrival and spread of the railways. This produced a new kind of capitalism, a distinctive American variety where the ethos centred firmly on the image of individual immigrant struggle. The world of US business was on its way. One of the most important changes which helped business success was population growth. The American population almost doubled in size between 1880 and 1910, and a large proportion of the increase was created by the new immigrants from Europe and the rest of the world. Success came from ambition and hard work, and anybody could make large amounts of money provided they tried hard enough. Helped by the success of some, immigrants flocked to the USA. By 1890, there were already over 4,000 American millionaires and Andrew Carnegie, who had made a fortune from railways and iron and steel, was spreading the "Gospel of Wealth". There were, however, some disadvantages to the new business environment. In many parts of the USA, there was more than an element of the Wild West. Con men, thieves and swindlers came to the new towns which were appearing, looking for suitable victims. A second major disadvantage was that Coke was originally a patent medicine, and only about two percent of the medicines which were produced ever became well-known – most inventors and salesmen failed miserably. Thirdly, although large profits could be made from all kinds of medicines, many of which often cost almost nothing to produce, by the late 1880s the market for medicines was already saturated. Patent medicines, therefore, were not an easy commercial area to break into. Another important aspect of the story is that the world of medicine was not advanced at this time. Nineteenth-century American doctors were not numerous, nor were they very good (anaesthetics were still to be invented and some of the primitive methods used by the medical profession were terrifying, killing more patients than they saved). This was the reason why many people turned to alternative remedies, the so-called patent medicines, to solve their health problems. By the end of the century, there were thousands of cures on offer for every imaginable ailment, from the common cold to malaria, all of which required extensive advertising in newspapers and public places to promote their superior values over their competitors. To conclude, it is not surprising that many would-be tycoons were attracted by the rising numbers of consumers and that the field of patent medicines was an attractive starting point for some. In 1869, Dr John Pemberton, a Georgia pharmacist, had moved to Atlanta searching to make his fortune by the discovery of the perfect patent cure. In 1886, after long years of research, he finally launched his new invention. It was into this very crowded and over-competitive market that Coca-Cola was to emerge as a highly successful product.

Task 2 Linking words and phrases

It is important to develop and link your ideas in each paragraph so the reader can follow your line of argument clearly. The Coca-Cola essay uses words and phrases to help the reader follow the sequence of events.

2.1 Match the words and phrases in the text that function in the same way as the following link words.

Firstly ....

Secondly ....

Thirdly ....

Fourthly ....

Finally ....

2.2 Look at the following link words and match them to their function.

> on the other hand   as shown by   for instance   in the same way   as a result
> equally important   like   another important aspect   therefore

Showing similarity ....

Comparing or contrasting ....

Adding something ....

Giving reasons ....

Showing cause and effect ....

Giving an example ....

Note: There is a large variety of link words and there are complex rules regarding their use. You should consult your tutor on a good source of reference to learn more about how to use them effectively.

Task 3 The topic sentence and supporting sentences

The topic sentence is usually at the beginning of a paragraph, but it does not have to be. When you write a paragraph, you should try to develop this initial idea and not change or add too many new ideas.

3.1 **Consider the following possible topic sentences for a paragraph on** The benefits of immigration to industrialised countries. **With another member of your group, discuss which sentence is most suitable.**

a)
> Immigration is a very difficult subject to discuss because there are many possible different viewpoints.

b)
> One of the major problems of immigration is that people in the host country may disagree with such a policy.

c)
> Immigration can offer several clear advantages for industrialised countries.

3.2 **Read the following two paragraphs. In each paragraph, the topic sentence has been underlined. Decide which paragraph develops the idea given in the topic sentence better. Discuss your reasons with your group.**

Example A
There are obvious advantages to learning English in Britain. Every day there are opportunities to practise listening to and speaking with British people. In the first place, students can experience the culture first-hand, which is a great help when trying to understand the language. This is especially true if they choose to live with a British family as exchange students, for example. In addition, if students attend a language school full-time, the teachers will be native speakers. In this case, not only will students' speaking and listening skills improve, but attention can be given to developing reading and writing skills as well.

Example B
Immigration to industrialised countries poses a number of difficult challenges for incoming families. They may need to learn a new language, they may face racism and discrimination and they frequently have problems adjusting to the new culture. In France, for example, it is illegal for Muslim schoolgirls to wear headscarves to school. Already, five Muslim schoolgirls have been expelled from school for wearing headscarves. The ban is perceived by many as intolerant, undermining the integration of France's Muslims. Feminists say the Islamic scarf is a repressive symbol, but many French Muslims say the ban is racist and against their human rights. "Everyone has the right to freedom of thought, conscience and religion; this right includes freedom to manifest their religion or belief in teaching, practice, worship and observance" (Article 18, The Universal Declaration of Human Rights).'

3.3 There are three thesis statements below. Write a topic sentence for each of them. Then write a supporting sentence or two for the paragraph. Remember to focus on the main idea. The first has been done for you.

A) Thesis statement — Young people who live at home while studying at university have several advantages.

Paragraph 1
Topic sentence — First of all, they can focus on their studies without worrying about domestic matters.

Supporting sentence(s) — Students living away from home have to learn how to do their own laundry and may well have to shop and cook for themselves. Those who live at home do not have such concerns.

B) Thesis statement
What is the focus here? — The causes and effects of global warming will be briefly outlined in this essay.

Paragraph 1
Topic sentence

Supporting sentence(s)

C) Thesis statement
What is the focus here? — Personal computers have revolutionised communication and business practices in the past twenty years.

Paragraph 1
Topic sentence

Supporting sentence(s)

20 Task: Essay Writing - Unit 3 - The body of the essay

Task 4 Organising an essay

4.1 Here are the opening words of the paragraphs from the original Coca-Cola essay in Task 1. Identify the topic and put the paragraphs into the correct order.

Paragraph begins	Topic	Order
Another important aspect of the story is that the world of medicine was not advanced at this time.		
There were, however, some disadvantages to the new business environment.		
To conclude, it is not surprising that many would-be tycoons were attracted by the rising numbers of consumers and that the field of patent medicines was an attractive starting point for some.		
One of the most important changes which helped business success was population growth.		
The first episode in the Coca-Cola story is an important part of the rise of capitalism in the United States of America.		

4.2 Look at the list of essay titles below. Discuss the following for each of them.

a) How would you structure your essay? e.g., *Reasons for and reasons against, causes followed by effects, problems followed by solutions*

b) What are the main points that you would include in the essay?

c) What sort of research will you have to do on this topic?

1) There is too much advertising on television.
2) Discuss the advantages and disadvantages of English as a world language.
3) How has education improved over the last one hundred years?
4) Marketing is the most important aspect of a business's activities. Discuss.
5) Every individual has a responsibility to prevent global warming.

4.3 Choose one title and make a plan for it, listing the topics you would cover in each paragraph.

4.4 Practise writing the first paragraph for your essay. Make sure you start with a clear topic sentence.

> **Reflect**
>
> When you understand how to structure an essay, you will begin to notice whether other writers have been successful in doing this well or not. By sharpening your critical skills, you will find your own writing skills will automatically grow.
>
> Look through examples of essays you or other students have written, with a view to developing your ability to recognise good organisation.

Student notes for Unit 3

Unit 4 Summaries and conclusions

At the end of this unit you will:
- have a clear idea of how to finish an academic essay with a successful conclusion.

The main aim of the conclusion is to show the reader that you have successfully answered the question that was set. It does not include any new information, but it summarises the main points made in the body of the essay. It should draw your argument to a close and it also needs to link back to the thesis statement in your introduction.

Task 1 Restating the thesis

You need to repeat the main ideas in the conclusion, but you do not want to simply write the same sentences again. One way of linking back to the thesis statement is to rewrite it (that is, to paraphrase the ideas and the language). You can use synonyms to do this, or you can rearrange the order and also change some of the grammar.

1.1 Look at the extract from an introduction below. Think of synonyms for the underlined words and write them in the table.

Lack of investment in public transport is having serious consequences for travellers in Britain today; this is the major point that will be discussed in this essay.

Original	Synonym
lack of	
consequences	
travellers	
major point	
discussed	

Unit 4 - Summaries and conclusions - Task: Essay Writing 23

1.2 Rewrite the sentence, using synonyms and different word order to make a good concluding statement. Think about the grammar that needs to change (e.g., *will be* is not appropriate for a conclusion).

Task 2 Organising the concluding paragraph

2.1 Rearrange the following sentences to form an effective conclusion for an essay on the topic of **Urban overcrowding**.

a) _____ Government policies aimed at solving these problems are too often very simple measures that offer only short-term solutions.

b) _____ In conclusion, urban overcrowding causes problems on all levels.

c) _____ It is a model which aims for improved social conditions and offers a high quality of life for city dwellers, whatever their number.

d) _____ This essay has argued for the implementation of a long-term policy which needs to provide an economically sustainable, resource-efficient model of city design.

e) _____ The creation of such a model will help to resolve many of the current and future problems of urban life.

Task 3 Finish with a clear statement

Remember that your conclusion needs to be clear and relevant to the question you are answering. A strong conclusion should refer back to the introduction. Ideally, it needs to leave a strong impression on the reader.

3.1 Read the following thesis statement and the concluding sentences of the same essay. Discuss the following questions.

a) What is the subject of the essay? Think of a title for it.

b) How is the conclusion similar to and different from the introduction?

Thesis statement: The growth of a 'fast food' culture in this country has generated unexpected problems, including rising obesity levels and, more importantly, the loss of our gastronomic heritage. This essay will examine the role of fast food in the development of an increasingly unhealthy Britain.

Conclusion: Fast food outlets cannot entirely be blamed for our increasingly unhealthy dietary habits. Fast food evidently responds to a need in our modern society, and reflects changes in our modern lifestyle. It is, rather, our lifestyle which needs changing if we hope to become a healthier nation.

3.2 Look back at the thesis statement you wrote in Unit 2, Task 4.3 (page 13), in which you stated the focus of your essay. Draw your argument to a close with a concluding sentence which refers back to your introduction. Try to use synonyms, paraphrases and different grammatical structures.

3.3 Sometimes it may be useful to draft a rough conclusion first, so that you know what you will say at the end of the essay. Can you think of any advantages or disadvantages of this approach? Discuss them and write them in the table.

Advantages	Disadvantages

Unit 4 - Summaries and conclusions - **Task: Essay Writing**

Task 4 Lecturer expectations

4.1 Tutors and lecturers have clear ideas of what they want to see in the conclusion to an academic essay. Look at the list below and check that you understand the expectations. Identify whether you think you are strong or weak in these areas.

Concluding: Lecturers expect ...	I am good, OK, weak at ...
clear links between the introduction and conclusion	
a strong concluding paragraph	
the ability to say the same thing in different ways (paraphrasing)	
accurate use of vocabulary	
accurate grammar	
a relevant concluding statement	
an answer to the question set (task completion)	

Reflect

You can make a comparison between writing a good conclusion and finishing other things you are faced with doing. Think about how satisfying it can be to complete a task to your satisfaction and how writing a good conclusion can be equally satisfying. Reflect on how the effort put into a conclusion will help you think more carefully about the assignment as a whole.

Look at an essay you or another student has written and think about how you can improve the conclusion to reflect the content of the essay. Think about how this process helps you focus on what the essay is saying.

Student notes for Unit 4

Unit 5: Academic style and register

At the end of this unit you will:
- be more familiar with the language of essays and able to identify some of the features of academic style;
- have practised using formal, objective language.

Task 1 Formal or informal register?

Academic essays usually require a formal style. You need to remember what to avoid in an academic essay.

1.1 Compare the following two definitions of Geography. Write the differences between them in the table below. Discuss your findings with a partner.

Informal/spoken: Geography? Well, I think it's basically just some sort of mix of physical and social sciences and how they interact together. You know, like, for example, how global warming has an effect on the economy, um, of a region … but you can also look at these things individually too … er … so you could just study things like sea-level rise which'd be physical, or you could look at … say … how people, human beings, adapt themselves to the environment, that's human.

Formal/written: Geography is the study of the surface of the Earth, the location and distribution of its physical and cultural features, and the interrelation of these features as they affect humans. In the study of geography, two main branches may be distinguished, physical geography and human geography.

Feature	Informal/spoken examples	Formal/written examples
Use of contractions, isn't, don't, etc.		
Use of fillers: Well, er, etc.		
Use of passive voice		
Impersonal and objective		
Personal and subjective		
Punctuation		

1.2   Do you notice any other features of formal or informal discourse in the texts? Add these features to the table.

1.3   Read the following sentences and decide if they are formal (F) or informal (I). Explain why, and add any further examples to the table above.

   a)   I don't believe this is true at all. It sounds like nonsense.
   b)   New regulations will come into effect next year.
   c)   The study was conducted with a group of school-age children.
   d)   We're definitely going to have to follow those stupid new rules next year.
   e)   Further analysis is required before conclusions can be drawn.
   f)   It really puzzles me why some students don't get better grades.
   g)   Our experiments were OK – they just proved that his argument didn't stand up.
   h)   He'll have to have a better look at the findings before making his mind up.
   i)   It has been proved that the claims are unfounded.
   j)   We went down to a school and chatted with some of the kids.
   k)   It isn't clear why quite a lot of students don't get really good grades.
   l)   A major aspect of the investigation involved research into social housing trends.

Task 2 Cautious language

Another typical feature of academic writing is the need to be careful or cautious. Unless you are quoting a fact or a statistic, or there is evidence which shows 100% certainty, statements and conclusions are often qualified in some way to make them less assertive or positive. The reason is partly English academic style, but it is also to avoid making any false claims. This use of cautious language is sometimes called 'hedging'.

2.1   Compare the following sentence pairs. What sort of language is used in the second sentence of each pair to make it less assertive or positive?

2.2   Underline the hedging expressions used in the second sentence of each pair and then write the example in the appropriate place in the table below. The first one has been done for you.

   A)   i)   Some colleges and universities in this country have large numbers of international students.
        ii   Some colleges and universities in this country appear to have large numbers of international students.

   B)   i)   Instead of coming here, international students should study in their own country.
        ii) It could be argued that, instead of coming here, international students should study in their own country.

   C)   i)   This is a misapplication of government policy.
        ii) This would seem to be a misapplication of government policy.

D) i) This is true.
　　ii) To a certain extent, this may be true.

E) i) Erlichman's findings prove that the amount of independent study is directly related to higher performance levels.
　　ii) Erlichman's findings suggest that the amount of independent study might be directly related to higher performance levels.

F) i) Inflation will not rise next year.
　　ii) Evidence indicates that inflation will probably not rise next year.

G) i) The survey demonstrates that English schoolchildren don't like learning more foreign languages.
　　ii) The survey tends to indicate that English schoolchildren are apparently not in favour of learning more foreign languages.

H) i) There are situations where this is the only solution.
　　ii) There are undoubtedly situations where this would seem to be the only possible solution.

Hedging feature	Example
hedging verbs	Some colleges ... appear to have ...
Use of modal verbs	
Qualifying expressions	
Adjectives and adverbs	
Set expressions	

Task 3 Register in use

Informal English uses everyday spoken forms (colloquialisms) that are inappropriate for formal written English. It is important not to mix styles in academic writing.

3.1 Here is a paragraph from the Coca-Cola essay you looked at earlier, rewritten in a much more informal style. Find and underline the parts that are too colloquial. Look particularly carefully at the vocabulary and the sentence structure.

A massive change – one which really helped business – was more people arriving in the USA. There were two times as many people who got here between 1880 and 1910, and lots of them came from all sorts of different places like Europe. If you wanted to be successful you had to work really hard; however, you could get rich quickly if you did this. Lots of immigrants made it and because of this, lots more wannabe millionaires turned up in the US. By 1890, America maybe had around 4,000 millionaires. One of the best was Andrew Carnegie, who got rich through trains and iron and steel. His message was called the 'Gospel of Wealth'.

3.2   Go back and check your answers with the original paragraph in Unit 3, Task 1.2.

3.3   The following extract from an essay is written in a mixed style with colloquialisms and other inappropriate words. Rewrite it in a more academic style using:

- appropriate vocabulary and grammatical structures;
- cautious language (Unit 5, Task 2, page 29).

Another kind of useful alternative fuel is electricity. This isn't really a very efficient fuel right now, because the technology is somewhat limited; however, it's fair to say that recent advances in the production of electric cars could maybe make this a reality in the future. But it is possible for cars powered with electricity to release little or no emissions, so if we want this alternative fuel to become a reality, we'll need it in lots of cars. Maybe then it'll make some sort of a difference. If we want this to happen, i.e., to knock a big chunk out of the pollution problem all around the world, it'll take a while.

Reflect

Read through an essay that you have recently written, looking carefully at the language you used. Bearing in mind what you have learned about the appropriate level of formality, do you feel that you could improve the way you express yourself?

Also check that the tone of the essay is not too assertive and explore whether it would benefit from more hedging expressions.

Student notes for Unit 5

Guidelines for the future

At the end of this unit you will:
- understand the editing and redrafting processes in essay writing;
- have a clearer understanding of what lecturers expect from a piece of academic writing.

Task 1 Things to remember

1.1 In Unit 1, Task 2, we looked at some basic principles. You should now be familiar with some of the main principles of essay writing. Check the following and decide which areas you will need to work on in the future.

- understanding the task
- checking the title carefully
- answering the question set
- getting organised
- keeping to deadlines
- writing a plan
- collecting and recording sources and important information
- keeping useful phrases and examples of 'essay language'
- reflecting on what you have written
- checking and redrafting language and content
- writing a final draft
- presenting your essay in a clear and acceptable form

Task 2 Redrafting

> source? Sp.   gr.   tense
> It was forcast that the number of robbery would have risen by 29% in london
>   wrong word
> between april 2001 and march 2002 but the real figures show that the overall
>   tense
> number of crimes was falling watch punctuation

Unit 6 - Guidelines for the future - Task: Essay Writing   33

2.1 Think about the answers to these two questions.

    a) How many drafts of an essay should you write?

    b) What do you need to consider and work on when you redraft an essay?

2.2 Make a list of the answers to 2.1 question b). Some examples are given below to help you.

Redrafting: things to work on	Considerations
paragraphs	• the right structure • each paragraph has a main idea • paragraphs are in the right order
grammar	
length of essay	

Task 3 How to get a better mark

Remember that your mark will depend not only on how good your writing is, but also on how successfully you have completed the task. It is important to make sure you read and understand the feedback that your lecturer gives you to help you with your next essay. It is also important to understand the marking criteria.

> For instance, robbery might be decreased whereas murder has increased so the total number of crimes has decreased. This is because the goverment always show their performance in a positive way.
>
> *Sp.*
> *good to include e.g.*
> *ref? – this is rather a generalisation!*

3.1 Here are some comments that lecturers sometimes make about students' writing. Which ones indicate that the lecturer thinks you have done what was required?

a) You have written a competent answer, but unfortunately it is an answer to a different question!

b) Your essay would be improved by checking the grammar and spelling.

c) You have answered the question very well; you show a good understanding of the issues and have provided some excellent examples.

d) There is little evidence in the essay of reflective and evaluative thought. Your conclusion is rather weak.

e) The essay needs to be word-processed – in general, the presentation is very poor.

f) You have made good use of personal reflection and have clearly done a lot of background reading on the topic.

g) You have described the situation well but have not analysed the advantages and disadvantages as the question asked you to do.

3.2 Can you add any other comments that teachers have made about your writing?

3.3 Look at the marking criteria on the following page for essay writing and match them with the appropriate percentage bands below (NB: 40% is the pass mark in this scheme).

| 70%+ |
| 60–69% |
| 50–59% |
| 40–49% |
| 30–39% |

Unit 6

Marking criteria	Mark
ideas generally not made clear and often irrelevant; weak paragraphs; small range of vocabulary; grammatical structure is very limited	
ideas generally clear but not always very relevant; some lack of paragraphing; limited range of vocabulary; limited grammatical structure at times	
lacks any satisfactory organisation or development of ideas; vocabulary use very weak; unsatisfactory use of grammatical structure; generally fails to meet the required pass standard	
excellent text organisation; clear paragraphs with well-expressed ideas; wide range of vocabulary; good use of grammatical structure	
good text organisation with generally relevant ideas; adequate range of vocabulary and grammatical structure	

Task 4 A model essay

4.1 Read the essay title below and underline the instruction verbs.

Essay title: Discuss the problems associated with urban overcrowding and evaluate possible solutions.

4.2 Read the introduction to the essay and answer the questions.

a) How does the writer arouse your interest?

b) What is the thesis statement?

Introduction:
The twentieth century saw a major increase in the world's population and at the same time the emergence of a global society driven by the forces of economics and industry. People were inexorably drawn towards living in towns and cities, migrating from rural communities out of economic necessity. As a result of this influx, modern-day cities across the globe face serious problems due to overcrowding. The most critical include poverty and homelessness, unemployment, the provision of adequate healthcare and education, and knock-on effects such as rising crime and pollution. The purpose of this essay is to identify solutions to some of these problems of urban overcrowding and attempt to evaluate their feasibility.

4.3 Now read the main body below and answer the questions that follow. Remember the introduction verbs in the essay title, and the thesis statement, while you read.

Main body:

Urban overcrowding is not a recent phenomenon, but it has recently become a global demographic problem. The rise of the world's 'Megacities' such as Tokyo, Jakarta, São Paulo and Cairo, with populations approaching 20 million, is one of the most marked trends of recent decades. In 1950 for example, New York City was unique among the world's cities in having more than 10 million inhabitants. By 1975 that number had grown to 15 million. By 2015 it is estimated it will reach 21 million. (UNO 2005). Two principal reasons for this phenomenon can be identified, one economic and the other sociocultural.

People migrate to the cities in search of both economic security and improved social conditions. As the economy of a nation develops, its cities develop as centres of industry, investment and education, providing plentiful job opportunities for those in search of a higher standard of living. Sydney, São Paulo and Frankfurt are all thriving modern cities which have developed exponentially since the Second World War. A further example is Tokyo, the hub for Japan's rapid economic development in the 1960s and 70s; its population grew quickly as people moved there to find employment, and it is now the most populous city in the world (population 35.3 million).

Not all developing nations, however, are equipped to cope with such rapidly expanding city populations. The overriding problem associated with overcrowding is poverty and its attendant social deprivations – homelessness, unemployment and insecurity. Immigrants to cities from rural areas are typically the poorest members of urban society, and in many cities are often forced to live in shantytowns or slums on the periphery of the city without access to clean drinking water or safe sanitation, in cramped and unsanitary conditions. Examples of such poor living conditions can be seen across the continents, from Caracas to Bombay. Unemployment is widespread as families fight to survive. Transmission of infectious diseases is very common in such conditions, resulting too frequently in high infant mortality rates (UNESCO 2002). Furthermore, access to vital social services such as hospitals and schools may be restricted as authorities try to cope with large numbers of people, thus denying children adequate education and healthcare.

Inevitably, there is no one best solution to a problem of such magnitude. Two solutions are proposed, both of which seek to move people away from the cities. The first is that of resettlement, where government-led housing initiatives seek to rehouse families on the outskirts of cities. The Shanghai housing resettlement project, begun in 1987, is an example of successful urban renewal where living conditions have been measurably improved. Resolution of the housing shortage has promoted long-term social development and stability, resulting in social and economic benefits. This measure does not, however, address the problem of urban sprawl as the city spreads outwards, but it does relieve the pressure of urban overcrowding.

The second solution encourages the relocation of businesses, factories and warehouses to rural areas. It exploits brownfield sites in the countryside which are developed as business parks. Policies of industrial relocation have been successful in Canada and the UK, where industrial expansion of cities has been curtailed. However, people are not willing to leave the cities unless they are guaranteed better housing, schools and transport facilities, so long-term government investment in these areas is crucial. Furthermore, such projects are disputed by environmentalists, who see the developments as a threat to the balance of the countryside.

a) Underline the topic sentence in each paragraph in the text and make a note of its key words below.

b) How much support does the writer give for the topic sentence in each paragraph? Make a note (key words) of the support below.

Paragraph 1
Topic sentence key words: Urban overcrowding = has become a global phenomenon

Support examples and evidence:

Paragraph 2
Topic sentence key words:

Support examples and evidence:

Paragraph 3
Topic sentence key words:

Support examples and evidence:

Paragraph 4
Topic sentence key words:

Support examples and evidence

Paragraph 5
Topic sentence key words:

Support examples and evidence:

Task: Essay Writing - Unit 6 - Guidelines for the future

4.4 Now compare your answers with another student. Decide which paragraph(s) do the following:

a) describe the situation and causes

b) suggest solutions

c) describe the problems

4.5 Read the conclusion and answer the questions below. (While you read, remember the important verbs in the essay title and the thesis statement in the introduction.)

a) Is there any new information in the conclusion?

b) How does the conclusion link back to the introduction?

Conclusion:
In conclusion, urban overcrowding causes problems on all levels. Government policies aimed at solving these problems are too often simple stopgap measures offering only short-term solutions. This essay has argued for the implementation of a long-term policy that potentially provides an economically sustainable, resource-efficient model of city design. It is a model that fulfils a universal desire for improved social conditions and ultimately offers a high quality of life for city dwellers, whatever their number.

4.6 Look through the whole essay and decide where you could make changes from assertive to more cautious hedging language. Write your changes in the table below.

Change from	To

Unit 6

Task 5 Write an essay outline

The sample essay in Task 1 was an example of the Situation-Problem-Solution-Response model (see Unit 3, page 17).

5.1 **Prepare an essay outline for the following essay question (or one of the other questions in this module). Follow the steps below.**

English has become a global language because it is both easy to learn and superior to other languages. Discuss.

- Analyse the question: How many general statements are there? What is the main instruction verb?
- Brainstorm ideas using one of the techniques from Unit 1, Task 3, page 19.

- Write a thesis statement to show how your argument will develop through the essay.
- Decide which essay pattern to use (Unit 3, page 20).
- Link your ideas into a logical sequence and decide how many paragraphs you will use.
- Write a topic statement for each paragraph.
- Note the supporting evidence and examples for each of your main points.
- Refer to TASK Module 10: *Research and Referencing*, if you are including quotations.

5.2 **Discuss your essay outlines in small groups.**

Reflect

You should now feel more confident about what is required in writing a formal academic essay. Think about your own skills and what you have learned in this unit. How will you use the information for the future? What do you need to do to become a better essay writer?

Student notes for Unit 6

40   Task: Essay Writing - Unit 6 - Guidelines for the future

Module 8

Web work

| Website 1 | ABC of academic writing and essays |

http://www.mdx.ac.uk/WWW/STUDY/gloess.htm#plans

Review
This is part of a guide for students at the University of Middlesex. It gives comprehensive explanations of terms and examples of essay types and sections.

Task
Note down useful words and terms connected with essay writing, together with their definitions.

| Website 2 | Andy Gillett's academic writing |

http://www.uefap.com/writing/writfram.htm

Review
This is a very useful study skills site written by Andy Gillett at the University of Hertfordshire.

Task
This link takes you to the writing section. Try the exercises at the end of each section, then check your answers. Begin with Understanding the Question and apply your knowledge from this module.

Extension activities

| Activity 1 | Write another essay outline |

Prepare an essay outline for the following essay question. Use the same steps as you did in Unit 6, Task 5:

Discuss the problems associated with the melting of the polar icecaps and evaluate possible solutions.

| Activity 2 | Write an essay |

Expand one of your essay outlines into a full essay. Although you may have a number of essays to write over the year, it is useful to write one immediately on completing this module.

You can complete one that you have been working on in this module, or choose an area to write about that you are particularly interested in.

Module 8

Glossary

Academic writing (n) Writing that students and academics produce. It normally involves research, demonstrates learning or knowledge and follows clear conventions in its style and organisation. For example, essays and assignments, reports, dissertations, theses.

Argument essay (n) An essay that involves building a case for an idea or thesis statement. This entails giving reasons for your thesis statement and providing evidence to back it up.

Analyse (v) To break an issue down into parts in order to study, identify and discuss their meaning and/or relevance.

Analytical essay (n) An essay that involves analysing a text, theory or set of ideas.

Brainstorm (v) The act of writing down all the thoughts and ideas you have about a topic without stopping to monitor, edit or organise them. Brainstorming is a creative process that can be done alone or in a group.

Colloquial (adj) Used to describe informal spoken words and expressions used in conversation, or informal written language used in letters to friends and family or e-mails. For example, in British English, a colloquial way of saying 'Don't be annoyed!' would be 'Don't get in a tizz!'

Deadline (n) The date or time by which an assignment or project needs to be completed.

Descriptive essay (n) An essay that describes a process or sequence of events rather than arguing, interpreting or evaluating.

Draft (n) (v) 1 (n) An early version of a piece of academic writing that is used as the starting point for further work. 2 (v) To create an early version of an essay, knowing that you will go back afterwards and develop and edit your language and ideas.

Edit (v) To select, rearrange and improve material to make it more suitable for its final purpose. Editing material involves reorganising it, correcting errors, improving the wording or content and changing its length, by adding sections or taking them out.

Evaluate (v) To assess information in terms of quality, relevance, objectivity and accuracy.

Evaluative essay (n) An essay that requires you to either compare and evaluate a range of things in relation to one another, or to look at the arguments for and against one thing, and come to a judgment in your conclusion. It is asking for your personal opinion, backed up with facts, examples and explanations.

Exemplify (v) To illustrate a belief, statement or theory with examples. You may be asked to do this in an essay.

Free writing (v) To write without deliberate or conscious thought so that ideas flow freely. This is sometimes done as an exercise to stimulate ideas and creativity in preparation for a written assignment.

Hedging (n) The use of deliberately vague, uncertain language in order to avoid asserting something as a fact that may not be true. In the context of academic writing, hedging language is often used to discuss theories and possible solutions.

Key skill (n) A skill that it is important to master in order to be successful in a certain area (such as academic life or employment).

Marking criteria (n) A list of criteria or qualities that the person who marks an assignment or exam is looking for, including aspects of the style, presentation and organisation of the work. For example, one criterion for an assignment that is graded above 70% (a first) is likely to be that it must include original ideas.

Mind map (n) A diagram used to represent words, ideas, tasks or other items linked to, and arranged radially around, a central key word or idea

Objective (adj) (n) 1 (adj) An opinion or idea that is not influenced by personal feelings or emotions. 2 (n) The aim, or what you want to achieve from an activity.

Outline (n) A brief plan that shows the order in which you will deal with the main issues or ideas in a piece of academic writing.

Paraphrase (v) To alter a piece of text so that you restate it (concisely) in different words without changing its meaning. It is useful to paraphrase when writing a summary of someone's ideas; if the source is acknowledged, it is not plagiarism. It is also possible to paraphrase your own ideas in an essay or presentation; that is, to state them again, often in a clearer, expanded way.

Personal experience essay (n) An essay that asks you to describe and draw conclusions about something that you have experienced.

Proofread (v) To read through a piece of writing and pick out and correct errors in it. It is useful to ask someone else to proofread your work. This should be done before the final draft of a piece of academic writing is submitted.

Redraft (v) To write out a new draft of an essay, incorporating changes and making additions. This is done after you have read through, edited and/or had feedback on the first draft.

Reference (n) (v) 1 (n) Acknowledgment of the sources of ideas and information that you use in written work and oral presentations. 2 (v) To acknowledge or mention the sources of information.

Reflective essay (n) An essay that involves thinking about a statement or idea and deciding whether you agree with it, and giving reasons for your decision.

Register (n) The style of speech or writing that is used in a specific context and/or by a specific group of people. For example, a student will use a very informal, colloquial register to text or e-mail a friend, but a formal scientific register to write a chemistry report.

Restate (v) To paraphrase or say something again in a different way. This is often done in essays to help clarify an idea or issue. The conclusion of an essay will often restate the original thesis statement in more depth.

Source (n) Something (usually a book, article or other text) that supplies you with information. In an academic context, sources used in essays and reports must be acknowledged.

Structure (n) (v) 1 (n) A framework or arrangement of several parts, put together in a particular way. 2 (v) In academic writing, to put together ideas, arguments or thoughts in an organised, logical way. It is important to structure essays and presentations as you work on them.

Subjective (adj) Describes an idea or opinion that is based on someone's personal opinion rather than on observable phenomena.

Supporting evidence (n) Information from academic sources that should be included in a piece of academic writing. This evidence illustrates and backs up your ideas and adds 'academic weight' to your work.

Supporting sentences (n) Sentences that usually follow and systematically develop the idea contained in the topic sentence.

Synonym (n) A word or phrase which has a similar meaning to another one and can replace it in a sentence without changing the meaning of the sentence.

Technique (n) A method or way of doing something. For example, it is possible to learn useful techniques for answering exam questions.

Thesis statement (n) A statement that explains the controlling idea or main argument (thesis) in a piece of academic writing. It is stated in the introduction and supported by reasons in the body of the essay.

Topic sentence (n) A sentence that states and sometimes summarises the topic/main idea of the paragraph and the standpoint taken by the writer. It usually comes at the beginning of each paragraph.

Further notes